COMPASS READING TEST SUCCESS

COMPASS TEST READING PRACTICE TESTS

Note: The Compass Test is a registered trademark of ACT Inc, which is not affiliated with nor endorses this publication.

TABLE OF CONTENTS

Compass Test Information

The Compass Test in reading is a placement test that your college will administer in order to assess your reading skills. The Compass is a computer-adaptive test. This means that you will take the test on a computer and that your response to previous questions will determine the difficulty level of subsequent questions.

Test questions on the Compass Test in reading are multiple-choice. When you take the actual test on the computer, the passage will appear on one side of the screen and the questions will appear on the other side.

For ease of reference, we have placed the passage on the left page and the questions on the right page in this book. For this reason, some pages have been left blank intentionally.

Since the Compass is a secure test, the items in this book are not actual test questions. However, this practice material is designed to simulate the reading level and format of questions you may face on the actual test.

Note: The Compass Test is a registered trademark of ACT Inc, which is not affiliated with nor endorses this publication

Reading Test 1

The Power of Tornadoes

Tornadoes are one of the most severe types of weather phenomena. While many people fear tornadoes and their destructive power, few people understand their real causes and effects, nor are they aware of how to protect themselves from their devastating force.

Tornadoes, violently rotating columns of air, occur when a change in wind direction, coupled with an increase in wind speed, results in a spinning effect in the lower atmosphere. These whirling movements, which may not be visible to the naked eye, are exacerbated when the rotating air column shifts from a horizontal to a vertical position. As the revolving cloud draws in the warm air that surrounds it at ground level, its spinning motion begins to accelerate, thereby creating a funnel that extends from the cloud above it to the ground below. In this way, tornadoes become pendent from low pressure storm clouds.

When a tornado comes into contact with the ground, it produces a strong upward draft known as a vortex, a spiraling column of wind that can reach speeds in excess of 200 miles per hour. Traveling across the landscape, the tornado wreaks a path of concentrated destruction. It is not uncommon for these twisters to lift heavy objects, like cars or large animals, and throw them several miles. Houses that succumb to the force of the tornado seem to explode as the low air pressure inside the vortex collides with the normal air pressure inside the buildings.

Tornadoes can occur at any time of the year, but are typically most frequent during the summer months. Equally, tornadoes can happen at any time during the day, but usually occur between 3:00 in the afternoon and 9:00 in the evening. While these fierce funnels occur in many parts of the world, they are most common in the United States. On average, there are 1,200 tornadoes per year in this vast nation, causing 70 fatalities and 1,500 injuries.

Although taking myriad shapes and sizes, tornadoes are generally categorized as weak, strong, or violent. The majority of all tornadoes are classified as weak, meaning that their duration is less than 10 minutes and they have a speed under 110 miles per hour. Comprising approximately 10 percent of all twisters, strong tornadoes may last for more than 20 minutes and reach speeds up to 205 miles per hour. Violent tornadoes are the rarest, occurring less than one percent of the time. While uncommon, tornadoes in this classification are the most devastating, lasting more than one hour and resulting in the greatest loss of life. That is why only violent tornadoes can completely destroy a well-built, solidly-constructed home, although weaker ones can also cause great damage.

1)   The word *pendent* in the passage is closest in meaning to
    A. revolving
    B. quickening
    C. hanging
    D. parallel
    E. dropping

2)   Which of the sentences below is the best paraphrase of the second sentence from paragraph 3?

      A. The tornado causes great damage to landscaped areas, such as parks and gardens.
      B. The tornado focuses its damage primarily upon localities that have been heavily landscaped.
      C. The tornado only causes damage to open areas, but the damage is usually very severe.
      D. As the tornado moves through the countryside, it causes extensive, geographically centralized damage.
      E. The tornado is able to destroy houses and move large objects.

3)   All of the following key facts about tornadoes are mentioned in the passage EXCEPT
      A. the number of deaths from tornadoes
      B. the time of day when tornadoes usually take place
      C. the time of year when tornadoes are most common
      D. the way in which tornadoes are classified
      E. the average wind speed of most tornadoes

4)   The word *myriad* in the passage is closest in meaning to
      A. limited
      B. extreme
      C. many
      D. average
      E. multiplied

5)   In paragraph 5, what is the author's main purpose?
      A. to explain how tornadoes are classified
      B. to identify the most frequent type of tornadoes
      C. to emphasize the loss of life and damage to property caused by tornadoes
      D. to compare weak tornadoes to strong tornadoes
      E. to demonstrate that tornadoes can result in fatalities

6)   According to the passage, tornadoes are considered to be a severe weather phenomenon because
      A. of the effects they create in the atmosphere.
      B. many people fear them.
      C. they produce strong vortexes.
      D. they can be placed into three discrete categories.
      E. they can result in death and devastation.

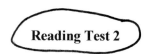

The Development of Professional Athletics

In my opinion, sports have long been a favorite pastime, if not a fanatical obsession, for Americans from all walks of life. Not only do sports exist as a source of entertainment for the American public, but also as a lucrative business enterprise for those who provide financial backing.

Let me give you one example. American Major League Baseball consisted of only a handful of teams when the National League was founded in 1876. It has grown in popularity by leaps and bounds over the years, resulting in increased ticket sales for games and bolstering the profits of its investors. The increased demand from the public, in turn, precipitated the formation of a new division, known as the American League, in 1901.

I should also say that new teams are formed from time to time in accordance with regional demand, such as the Colorado Rockies in Denver, Colorado, and the Devil Rays in Tampa Bay, Florida.

But, I think we can all agree that the sport which has reaped the largest monetary benefit has been American basketball. Successful marketing, together with the aggressive recruitment of new players, has helped to enthrall Americans with this sport. With hindsight, it appears that the National Basketball Association (NBA) made the big time in the late 1980's when several new teams were set up. Previously existing teams, such as the Chicago Bulls, also experienced an increase in popularity during this era.

1) Who is most likely to be conveying this information?
   A. a child
   B. an uninformed member of the public
   C. a college professor
   D. a sports commentator
   E. a football player

2) Sports in America
   A. exist solely due to the demand for entertainment displayed by the public.
   B. have become popular only because of monetary assistance provided by various companies.
   C. are profitable for the public.
   D. are enjoyable for Americans from various strata of society.
   E. have become popular only recently.

3) The popularity of American baseball
   A. was doomed from the beginning.
   B. is a result of successful marketing.
   C. has experienced rapid periodic growth.
   D. is due to the establishment of new teams.
   E. is exemplified by the Chicago Bulls.

4) New baseball teams are established as a result of
   A. regulations of the league.
   B. increased ticket sales.
   C. a reduction in financial support from investors.
   D. the interest displayed by the members of the public in a particular geographical area.
   E. the boundaries of a league being extended.

5) Which factor contributed to the increased popularity of American basketball?
   A. new investors
   B. cunning marketing.
   C. employment of new players.
   D. both (B) and (C).
   E. (A), (B) and (C).

6) Which of the following statements is true according to the passage?
   A. All Americans enjoy baseball.
   B. By examining the past, we can see that the formation of new teams made basketball successful.
   C. The American and National Leagues were formed due to a slump in regional markets.
   D. A higher volume of ticket sales depends upon larger investor expenditures.
   E. The Colorado Rockies team is the newest one in its division.

Reading Test 3

Oliver Twist

Oliver, having taken down the shutters, was graciously assisted by Noah, who having consoled him with the assurance that "he'd catch it," condescended to help him. Mr. Snowberry came down soon after.

Shortly afterwards, Mrs. Snowberry appeared. Oliver having "caught it," in fulfilment of Noah's prediction, followed the young gentleman down the stairs to breakfast.

"Come near the fire, Noah," said Charlotte. "I have saved a nice little bit of bacon for you from master's breakfast."

"Do you hear?" said Noah.

"Lord, Noah!" said Charlotte.

"Let him alone!" said Noah. "Why everybody lets him alone enough, for the matter of that."

"Oh, you queer soul!" said Charlotte, bursting into a hearty laugh. She was then joined by Noah, after which they both looked scornfully at poor Oliver Twist.

Noah was a charity boy, but not a workhouse orphan. He could trace his geneology back to his parents, who lived hard by; his mother being a washerwoman, and his father a drunken soldier, discharged with a wooden leg, and a diurnal pension of twopence-halfpenny and an unstable fraction. The shop boys in the neighbourhood had long been in the habit of branding Noah, in the public streets, with the ignominious epithets of "leathers," "charity," and the like; and Noah had borne them without reply. But now that fortune had cast his way a nameless orphan, at whom even the meanest could point the finger of scorn, he retorted on him with interest.

Adapted from *Oliver Twist* by Charles Dickens

1.   What is the meaning of "he'd catch it" in the first paragraph of the passage?
     A. he'd find it
     B. he'd buy it
     C. he'd be saved
     D. he would be laughed at
     E. he would be punished

2.   According to the passage, Oliver could be described as
     A. gracious
     B. scornful
     C. ignominious
     D. esteemed
     E. ridiculed

3.   The passage mainly illustrates
     A. Charlotte's contempt of orphans.
     B. the wealth of the Snowberry family.
     C. the exploits of Oliver Twist.
     D. Noah's childhood experiences.
     E. the relationship between Noah and Oliver.

4.   Who is the "nameless orphan" mentioned in the passage?
     A. charity boys
     B. workhouse orphans
     C. Noah
     D. Oliver
     E. Charlotte

5.   Who is telling this story?
     A. a third-person narrator
     B. Oliver
     C. Noah
     D. Charlotte
     E. Mr. Snowberry

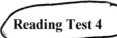

Television Networks and Broadcasting

When people are bored or have too much time on their hands, an easy solution is readily available: simply turn on the tube. One thing for certain is that Americans are constantly being accosted by an overabundance of television programs.

Today Americans have three national networks from which to choose: the American Broadcasting Corporation (ABC); the National Broadcasting Corporation (NBC), and the Columbia Broadcasting System (CBS). These networks broadcast programs free of charge to the public, relying on the support of major American commercial enterprises, such as Coca-Cola and Kimberly Clark, in the form of airtime purchased to advertise their products.

Commercial support is, by and large, intertwined with the public's often temperamental viewing preferences. The Nielsen Ratings are statistical indicators which measure such viewing trends by evaluating how many families are watching a certain program on a given network during a particular day or time. If the Nielsen Rating for a certain program is too low, a potential advertiser will be reluctant to purchase airtime during its broadcast as the advertising message will not reach the maximum number of viewers.

Firms will reach the largest audience during what is known as "Prime Time," the window of advertising opportunity from 7:00 P.M. to 10:00 P.M. Taking the volume of viewers into account, commercial entities devour this airtime with alacrity. A plethora of popular situation comedies, known as sit-coms, are aired during these evening hours. Other commercial opportunities exist during morning and afternoon broadcasts of long-running talk shows, game shows, and soap operas, now euphemistically termed "daytime dramas."

1) Which of the following statements concerning national networks is false?
   A. Networks are reliant upon businesses for monetary support.
   B. The network's success depends solely upon the public's viewing habits.
   C. The national network is also known as the National Broadcasting Corporation.
   D. Families do not pay a fee to watch national television.
   E. Television is a common remedy for boredom.

2) Television programs
   A. are few and far between.
   B. are broadcast during purchased airtime.
   C. are constantly being altered.
   D. are more frequent during Prime Time.
   E. provide Americans with more than enough options from which to choose.

3) The public's viewing habits
   A. are assessed by the Nielsen Ratings.
   B. are constant and unwavering.
   C. are influenced by advertising.
   D. fluctuate in relation to commercial support.
   E. are influenced by Coca-Cola.

4) An advertiser will communicate his message to the largest amount of viewers
   A. when the Nielsen Rating increases.
   B. during daytime dramas.
   C. during the evening hours.
   D. in the morning.
   E. in the afternoon.

5) Commercial opportunities are
   A. most plentiful during the broadcast of soap opera episodes.
   B. at their zenith during game shows.
   C. thwarted by statistical ratios compiled by Nielsen.
   D. the best during Prime Time.
   E. greater during the morning than during the afternoon.

Reading Test 5

Mount Rushmore in the Black Hills

In the Black Hills in the state of South Dakota in the United States, four visages protrude from the side of a mountain. The faces are those of four United States' presidents: George Washington, Thomas Jefferson, Theodore Roosevelt, and Abraham Lincoln. Overseen and directed by the Danish-American sculptor John Gutzon Borglum, the work on this giant display of outdoor art was a Herculean task that took 14 years to complete.

A South Dakota state historian named Doane Robinson originally conceived of the idea for the memorial sculpture. He proposed that the work be dedicated to popular figures, who were prominent in the western United States and accordingly suggested statues of western heroes such as Buffalo Bill Cody and Kit Carson. Deeming a project dedicated to popular heroes frivolous, Borglum rejected Robinson's proposal. It was Borglum's firm conviction that the mountain carving be used to memorialize individuals of national, rather than regional, importance.

Mount Rushmore therefore became a national memorial, dedicated to the four presidents who were considered most pivotal in US history. Washington was chosen on the basis of being the first president. Jefferson, who was of course a president, was also instrumental in the writing of the American Declaration of Independence. Lincoln was selected on the basis of the mettle he demonstrated during the American Civil war, Roosevelt for his development of Square Deal policy, as well as being a proponent of the construction of the Panama Canal. Commencing with Washington's head first, Borglum quickly realized that it would be best to work on only one head at a time, in order to make it compatible with its surroundings. In order to help him visualize the final outcome, he fashioned a 1.5 meter high plaster model on a scale of 1 to 12.

Work on the venture began in 1927 and was completed in 1941. The cost of the project was nearly $1,000,000, which was raised mostly from national government funds, and also from charitable donations from magnanimous and benevolent members of the public. The carving of the mountain was tedious and arduous work, employing 360 men who worked in groups of 30. The daily working conditions on the mountainside can best be described as treacherous. For instance, men were often strapped inside leather harnesses that dangled over the cliff edge. Workers needed great strength to withstand the exertion of drilling into the mountainside.

The workmen faced frequent delays due to a dearth of financial backing in the early days, in addition to inclement weather throughout the 14 year period. Adverse conditions were also discovered when the carving of Jefferson began. The detection of poor quality stone on the mountain to the left of Washington resulted in Jefferson's face being repositioned to the right side. In spite of these setbacks, Mount Rushmore remained the best choice for the venue of the memorial. Yet, a large amount of the rock had to be blasted away from the mountain using dynamite or pneumatic drills, and as a result, approximately 450,000 tons of rock still lies at the foot of the mountain today.

1) The word *visage* in this passage is closest in meaning to
   A. body
   B. nose
   C. head
   D. face
   E. expression

2) The word *frivolous* in this passage is closest in meaning to
   A. unimportant
   B. serious
   C. expensive
   D. unwanted
   E. stupid

3) According to the passage, all of the following statements about Mount Rushmore are true EXCEPT:
   A. The project was predominantly funded on a federal level.
   B. Generous private individuals contributed financial backing for the work.
   C. Funding was plentiful at the beginning of the project.
   D. Adverse weather conditions sometimes hampered work on the project.
   E. A massive about of labor and effort was expended on the project.

4) The word *venue* in this passage is closest in meaning to
   A. rock
   B. mountain
   C. site
   D. consideration
   E. position

5) Why did Doane Robinson suggest that the western heroes be the subject of the monument?
   A. Western heroes were well-known and loved by the public.
   B. The westward expansion movement would not have been successful without Buffalo Bill Cody and Kit Carson.
   C. Such figures were of national import.
   D. The dedication of a sculpture to Western heroes would raise their profiles.
   E. They had a high level of notoriety.

6) Based solely on the information contained in paragraphs 2 and 3 of the passage, which of the following statements about the selection of presidents for Mount Rushmore is TRUE?
   A. There was some debate about which presidents to choose.
   B. These four presidents were well known internationally.
   C. These presidents changed the course of US policy and history.
   D. These presidents were of some importance regionally.
   E. It was not necessary to use a scale model for this project.

7)   Why was it necessary to change the location of the carving for Jefferson?
     A. because of poor weather
     B. due to a lack of money
     C. because the rock on the original location was of inferior condition
     D. since Borglum changed his mind
     E. because of his involvement in the Declaration of Independence

8)   Which of the following statements accurately expresses the author's attitude about John Gutzon Borglum and his work?
     A. He was a talented and perceptive artist.
     B. He was profligate in his spending for the Mount Rushmore project.
     C. His work was misunderstood during his lifetime.
     D. He was an incompetent craftsman.
     E. His work is an inappropriate legacy.

This page has been left blank intentionally.

The American Educational System

Working parents have recently prompted widespread growth in the American educational system. It is now common for children from both middle-class and well-to-do families to begin nursery school at the age of two. Most parents also seize the opportunity to send their children to pre-school subsequent to nursery school. Neither of these educational programs, which are operated independently by private organizations, are mandatory. In fact, state-sponsored education is not usually compulsory until the child is five years old. At this time, the child is required to attend kindergarten at the public elementary school in the district where his parents reside. The child will normally remain at elementary school until the sixth grade. However, prodigious students may advance more quickly if given the go-ahead by the school principal.

Junior high or middle school, which generally comprises the seventh and eighth grades, commences after the completion of elementary school. During these years, the student is not only compelled to attend normal academic courses, but also has the prerogative to choose from a wide range of extra-curricular activities, such as musical groups and athletic teams.

Non-academic activities remain prevalent throughout high school, which follows junior high school. Yet, some parents view these activities as a hindrance to the learning process. Indeed, students with aspirations of going to college must size up their academic program quite carefully during this educational period. Most students will solicit the advice of the school's academic guidance counselor to receive information about the admissions criteria of various colleges, as well as to seek help in registering for one of the two most popular existing college admissions tests: the American College Test (ACT) or the Scholastic Aptitude Test (SAT). On the other hand, students without the drive to attend college upon graduation may choose to partake in various vocational courses offered through the high school, such as sewing or automotive repair.

1)   Nursery and pre-school programs
         A. are required by the state government.
         B. are operated only by charities.
         C. are attended by children from various economic levels of society.
         D. have developed slowly over time.
         E. have been established by working parents.

2)   Which of the following statements concerning elementary school is true?
         A. Before attending elementary school, a child is required to attend pre-school.
         B. Parents can choose which elementary school their child will attend.
         C. Intellectually gifted students can be promoted if given approval by the principal.
         D. A child must attend public elementary school before attending kindergarten.
         E. Profligate students can skip a grade.

3)   According to the passage, during junior high school
         A. it is necessary for a student to participate in non-academic activities.
         B. students can be expelled for tardiness.
         C. students should make a tentative decision about attending college.
         D. students are required to attend the set curriculum.
         E. most students participate in music or sports.

4)   The Scholastic Aptitude Test
         A. is taken in conjunction with the American College Test.
         B. is obligatory for students with vocational orientations.
         C. is administered by an academic guidance counselor.
         D. is an alternative to the American College Test.
         E. is the most popular college admissions test.

5)   Students who do not wish to attend college
         A. need to consult with the school guidance counselor.
         B. are more strongly encouraged to participate in after-school activities.
         C. can attend classes to obtain work-related training.
         D. must take the ACT.
         E. must take the SAT.

Reading Test 7

Gravity and the Mechanics of Motion

The question of the mechanics of motion is complex and one that has a protracted history. Indeed, much has been discovered about gravity, defined as the force that draws objects to the earth, both before and since the British mathematician Sir Isaac Newton mused upon the subject in the 17th century. As early as the third century BC, a Greek philosopher and natural scientist named Aristotle conducted a great deal of scientific investigation into the subject. In fact, most of Aristotle's life was devoted to the study of the objects of natural science, and it is for this work that he is most renowned. The Greek scientist wrote a tome entitled *Metaphysics*, which contains the observations that he made as a result of performing this original research in the natural sciences.

Several centuries later, in the first century AD, Ptolemy, another Greek scientist, was credited with a nascent, yet unformulated theory, that there was a force that moved toward the center of the earth, thereby holding objects on its surface. Although later ridiculed for his belief that the earth was the centre of the planetary system, Aristotle's compatriot nevertheless did contribute to the development of the theory of gravity.

However, it was during the period called the renaissance that gravitational forces were perhaps studied most widely. An astronomer, Galileo Galilei corrected one of Aristotle's erring theories by pointing out that objects of differing weights fall to earth at the same speed. Years later, Descartes, who was known at that time as a dilettante philosopher, but was later dubbed the father of modern mathematics, held that a body in circular motion strives to constantly recede from the centre. This theory added weight to the notion that bodies in motion had their own forces.

Newton took these studies a step further and used them to show that the earth's rotation does not fling bodies into the air because the force of gravity, measured by the rate of falling bodies, is greater than the centrifugal force arising from the rotation. In his first mathematical formulation of gravity, published in 1687, Newton posited that the same force that kept the moon from being propelled away from the earth also applied to gravity at the earth's surface. While this finding, termed the Law of Universal Gravitation, is said to have been occasioned by Newton's observation of the fall of an apple from a tree in the orchard at his home, in reality, the idea did not come to the scientist in a flash of inspiration, but was developed slowly over time.

Newton had the prescience to appreciate that his study was of great import for the scientific community and for society as a whole. It is because of Newton's work that we currently understand the effect of gravity on the earth as a global system. For instance, as a result of Newton's investigation into the subject of gravity, we know today that geological features such as mountains and canyons can cause variances in the Earth's gravitational force. Newton must also be acknowledged for the realization that the force of gravity becomes less robust as the distance from the equator diminishes, due to the rotation of the earth, as well as the declining mass and density of the planet from the equator to the poles.

Yet, throughout his lifetime, Newton remained perplexed by the causes of the power implied by the variables of his mathematical equations on gravity. In other words, he was unable adequately to explain the natural forces upon which the power of gravity relied. Even though he tried to justify these forces by describing them merely as phenomena of nature, differing hypotheses on these phenomena still abound today.

1) The word *renowned* in the passage is closest in meaning to
   A. despised
   B. famous
   C. welcomed
   D. important
   E. significant

2) The word *nascent* in the Test is closest in meaning to
   A. newly formed
   B. old fashioned
   C. widely accepted
   D. obviously untrue
   E. re-born

3) The phrase *Aristotle's compatriot* in paragraph 2 refers to
   A. Metaphysics
   B. the planetary system
   C. Ptolemy
   D. an unformulated theory
   E. Ptolemy's theories

4) Which of the sentences below is the best paraphrase of paragraph 4?
   A. Newton created his Law of Universal Gravitation immediately after he observed an apple falling from a tree in his orchard.
   B. The Law of Universal Gravitation, while similar on occasion to falling apples, is usually the result of observing objects which fall more slowly to earth.
   C. Newton's law of gravity was not the result of a single observation of a fruit tree, but rather was created over many years.
   D. Stories about Newton's observance of falling apples are based on fact, rather than folklore, because of the time-consuming process of the theories relating to these stories.
   E. The absence of gravity would cause objects to be flung mid-air.

5) The word *prescience* in the Test is closest in meaning to
   A. pre-scientific
   B. hindsight
   C. investigation
   D. perception
   E. research

6) All of the following key facts about gravity are mentioned in paragraph 5 EXCEPT
    A. the effect of geology upon gravitational forces
    B. the impact of the varying density of the earth on gravity
    C. the manner in which gravitational force becomes weaker near the equator
    D. the way in which gravity influences rock formations
    E. how the spinning of the earth affects gravity

7) In paragraph 6, what is the author's main purpose?
    A. to emphasize the significance of Newton's achievement
    B. to identify a reservation which Newton experienced
    C. to analyze natural phenomena
    D. to highlight Newton's incompetence
    E. to reconcile various gravitational theories

8) According to the Test, what statement best describes Aristotle?
    A. He was the founder of the Law of Universal Gravitation
    B. He was best-known for producing error-free work.
    C. He was a physicist.
    D. He was a famous Greek natural scientist.
    E. He was a contemporary of Ptolemy.

9) Descartes was celebrated for establishing what subject?
    A. mathematics
    B. natural science
    C. astronomy
    D. philosophy
    E. physics

10) Select the answer below that represents the most important idea contained in the Test.
    A. The study of the mechanics of motion has endured for many centuries.
    B. Ptolemy is one of the most famous natural scientists.
    C. Newton's study of gravitational forces was of invaluable significance.
    D. The strength of gravitational force is directly related to the distance to the equator.
    E. Newton was confused by the power from which gravity was derived.

This page has been left blank intentionally.

Reading Test 8

The Theories of Jean Piaget

Born in France in 1896, Jean Piaget became one of the most influential thinkers in the areas of education psychology and child development in the twentieth century. The primary thrust of his research revolved around the question: "How do human beings come to know?" His research culminated in the groundbreaking discovery of what he called "abstract symbolic reasoning." The basic idea behind this principle was that biology influences child development to a greater extent than does socialization. That is to say, Piaget concluded that younger children answered research questions differently than older ones not because they were less intelligent, but because their intelligence was at a lower stage of biological development.

Because he was a biologist, Piaget had a keen interest in the adaptation of organisms to their environment, and this preoccupation led to many astute observations. Piaget found that behavior in children was controlled by mental organizations called "schemes," which enable an individual to interpret his or her world and respond to situations. Piaget coined the term "equilibration" to describe the biological need of human beings to balance these schemes against the processes of environmental adaptation.

The French-born biologist postulated that schemes are innate since all children are born with these drives. Noting that while other animals continued to deploy their in-born schemes throughout the entire duration of their lives, Piaget hypothesized that human beings' pre-existing, innate schemes compete with and ultimately diverge from constructed schemes, which are socially-acquired in the environmental adaptation process.

As Piaget's research with children progressed, he identified four stages of cognitive development. In the first stage, which he termed the sensorimotor stage, Piaget noted that at the incipience of the child's mental development, intelligence is displayed by way of the infant's physical interactions with the world. That is, the child's intelligence is directly correlated to his or her mobility and motor activity. Children begin to develop some language skills, as well as memory, which Piaget called "object permanence," during this initial stage.

When the child becomes a toddler, he or she enters the pre-operational stage. During this stage the child is largely egocentric, meaning that intellectual and emotional energy is directed inwardly, rather than on other individuals. Although memory, language, and intelligence continue to develop during these years, thinking is illogical and inflexible on the whole.

Next, the child begins the concrete operational stage. Beginning roughly at age 5, this stage is characterized by the appearance of logical and systematic thought processes. In this stage, the child begins to conceptualize symbols and measurements relating to concrete objects, such as numbers, weights, lengths, and volumes. As the child's intelligence becomes more logical, egocentrism begins to dissipate.

At the commencement of the teenage years, the final stage, called the formal operational stage, is initiated. During this stage, the individual should be able to grasp abstract thought on a range of complex ideas and theories. Yet, unfortunately, recent research has shown that adults in many countries around the globe have failed to complete this stage, perhaps owing to poverty or poor educational opportunities.

1) Based on the information in paragraph 1, which of the following best explains the term *abstract symbolic reasoning*?
   A. The idea that younger children are less intelligent that older children.
   B. The idea that younger children are less physically developed than older children.
   C. The idea that younger children are less socially developed than older children.
   D. The idea that younger children are less culturally developed than older children.
   E. The idea that biological development affects the intellectual development of children.

2) The word *coined* in the passage is closest in meaning to
   A. discovered
   B. evaluated
   C. created
   D. realized
   E. introduced

3) According to paragraph 2, all of the following are accurate statements about Piaget EXCEPT:
   A. Piaget's views as a biologist affected his work on child development.
   B. Piaget discovered that the child's biological development is connected to his or her mental functioning.
   C. Piaget noted that environmental factors played a role in child development, as well as biological factors.
   D. Piaget's research observations were apropos.
   E. Piaget was the first scientist to investigate child development.

4) The word *incipience* in the passage is closest in meaning to
   A. beginning
   B. early stage
   C. cognition
   D. interaction
   E. onset

5) The word *egocentric* in the passage is closest in meaning to
   A. extroverted
   B. self-centered
   C. illogical
   D. underdeveloped
   E. undisciplined

6) Which of the sentences below contains the main idea of paragraph 3?
   A. Piaget theorized that, unlike the schemes of other animals, human being's schemes are primarily acquired in the socialization process.
   B. In contrast to other animals, human beings use their innate schemes throughout their lifetimes, rather than departing from constructed schemes.
   C. The process by which human beings acquire schemes is different than that of other animals because human beings acquire schemes during the socialization process, and these acquired schemes bifurcate from their innate schemes.
   D. Piaget noted that human beings differ to other animals since they do not rely only on in-born cognitive mechanisms.
   E. Piaget theorized that children's schemes are completely socially acquired.

7) According to the passage, which of the following statements best characterizes the sensorimotor stage?
   A. The growth of the child's intelligence in this stage depends predominantly on his or her verbal ability.
   B. The skills obtained during this stage are of less importance than those achieved during later developmental stages.
   C. During this stage, the child learns how his or her mobility relates to language.
   D. The child's interaction with the world is limited.
   E. The child's cognitive development in this stage is achieved through physical movement in his or her environment.

8) Based on the information in paragraphs 5 and 6, what can be inferred about child development?
   A. Before the child enters the concrete operational stage, his or her thinking is largely rigid and unsystematic.
   B. The conceptualization of symbols is not as important as the conceptualization of numbers.
   C. The child becomes more egocentric during the concrete operational stage.
   D. Memory and language become less important during the concrete operational stage.
   E. The child develops by psychologically interacting with others during the pre-operational stage.

9) According to the passage, the formal operational stage
   A. is the result of poor economic conditions.
   B. has not yet been finished by many individuals around the world.
   C. is an important global problem.
   D. is based on complicated scientific theories.
   E. in no way is connected to the availability of education.

This page has been left blank intentionally.

Reading Test 9

Motion Picture Production

The motion picture industry, located in the heart of Hollywood, California, produces thousands of motion pictures a year. Although the movie-making process appears effortless when the movie is released to the viewing public, the process is, in reality, lengthy, time-consuming, and expensive.

The first step is to obtain the movie script, which is usually procured from the Screen Writers' Guild. Since the strength of the story can make or break the production, movies with underdeveloped or disjointed plots are automatically refused.

The next step is to find a producer who is capable of obtaining the monetary endowment of a major motion picture company for the movie's production. Companies such as Touchstone and Paramount are currently among the forerunners in the motion picture production industry.

Of course, the undertaking will not materialize without the input of a director. Actors perform under the auspices of the director, and they must refrain from doing anything which he or she prohibits. Stunt men and women are also employed to perform any tasks that would endanger the safety of the actors.

In addition, the cinematography must be considered. The special effects team is responsible for all adornments of the movie, from the plain and simple to the elaborate and extravagant. The camera crew works in close cooperation with the special effects team to reproduce the contrived result. *Matrix Revolutions*, which contains some of the most colossal special effects of any movie ever produced, is an example of the successful collaboration of computerized special effects and effective camera work.

The momentous event of releasing the movie to the public follows the production process. While critics may play a small role in the popularity of the movie, its success ultimately lies with its acceptance by the movie-going public.

1)   Which statement is true according to the passage?
   A. The movie script must originate from the Screen Writers' Guild.
   B. Productions of stories with intricate plots will receive only minimal monetary support from the motion picture company.
   C. The producer is responsible for winning financial backing from the motion picture company.
   D. Touchstone and Paramount are the best motion picture companies in Hollywood.
   E. The production of only a few movies becomes protracted.

2)   It is the responsibility of the director to
   A. co-ordinate the camera crew and the special effects team.
   B. make all decisions concerning cinematography.
   C. determine which script will be produced.
   D. provide guidance to the actors.
   E. obtain the movie script.

3)   The special effects team
   A. must not contravene the wishes of the director.
   B. usually produces magnificent cinematographic results.
   C. must work in synchronization with the camera crew.
   D. assigns tasks to stunt men and women.
   E. cooperates with the actors.

4)   The popularity of a movie is mainly dependent on
   A. the opinions of critics.
   B. members of the public who attend movies.
   C. the speed of the production process.
   D. the assistance provided by the motion picture industry.
   E. the volume of advertising.

5)   Which statement is false according to the passage?
   A. Movie scripts are normally obtained from the motion picture company.
   B. Actors must behave in accordance with the wishes of the director.
   C. The special effects team strives to re-create an agreed-upon design.
   D. The final step in the production process is the release of the movie.
   E. Most movies are costly to produce.

6)   Why does the author mention *Matrix Revolutions*?
   A. to illustrate cinematography
   B. to explain movie adornments
   C. to criticize the camera crew
   D. to describe how complicated special effects are produced
   E. to exemplify how special effects and camera work can be best combined

Reading Test 10

The Automotive Industry and Buyer Preference

When an individual driver tries to decide which new car to buy, he or she considers not only the price range of the vehicle. Personal preferences and a host of individual idiosyncrasies also come into play.

Buyers classified as affluent may contemplate purchasing a sleek new Lincoln Continental. Being spacious enough to seat six passengers comfortably, this automobile is seen as a status symbol that serves to flaunt the wealth of its owner.

Those purchasers with more garish tastes may prefer a Cadillac or perhaps a Chrysler New Yorker. These exclusive models are as roomy as the Continental and also provide the owner with a tangible, conspicuous means to display his or her affluence.

Individuals who are not as highly remunerated in their careers may wish to make a less audacious purchase, however. The line of contemporary Buick models may be an option for these car buyers. The lack of an imposing sticker price makes these models a shrewd choice for individuals with less stuffy personalities.

Yet, the prices of all of these models may present obstacles to those consumers beset with financial problems. Many American people consider a car to be an indispensable necessity for their day-to-day activities, but they simply cannot afford to patronize the expensive dealerships.

Plymouth and Chevrolet have found an innovative and ingenious solution to this dilemma: the compact car. Most consumers, even those earning a pittance, can afford compact models such as the Neon and Metro since they are not as luxurious as Cadillacs or New Yorkers.

1) The kind of vehicle a consumer purchases
   A. is determined solely by the invoice price.
   B. is mainly influenced by a particular buyer's quirks.
   C. is directly related to the customer's wealth.
   D. depends on personal preference
   E. is influenced by a number of factors.

2) The Lincoln Continental
   A. can accommodate more passengers that a Cadillac.
   B. is more ostentatious than a New Yorker.
   C. is usually acquired by customers who are categorized as well-to-do.
   D. is currently the most expensive model on the market.
   E. is the most comfortable car on the market.

3) Which of the following statements is true according to the passage?
   A. The interior dimensions of a New Yorker are roughly equivalent to those of a Continental.
   B. A Buick is more expensive than a Cadillac.
   C. The Chevrolet Metro is the most popular model nowadays.
   D. Highly compensated professionals prefer the Plymouth Neon.
   E. The Neon and Metro are status symbols.

4) The new range of vehicles manufactured by Buick
   A. are more affordable than some produced by Chrysler.
   B. often have a prohibitive price tag.
   C. are generally selected by pretentious customers.
   D. display the prestige of their owner.
   E. are more ostentatious than Cadillacs.

5) The new lines of compact cars
   A. have created a dilemma for car buyers.
   B. are quite cheap, but prone to problems.
   C. can be purchased by consumers with low incomes.
   D. are sold only by elite dealerships.
   E. are the most popular nowadays.

Reading Test 11

Crime and Punishment

Many steps are required in successfully prosecuting a criminal case in the American legal system. Once the crime has been committed and discovered, the police force is dispatched to the crime scene to begin the investigation. Simultaneously, any possible suspects or witnesses are taken in for questioning at the local police precinct having jurisdiction over the case.

Suspects and witnesses can be subjected to mild inquisition or full-scale interrogation, depending upon the severity of the matter. During this time, suspects might be held in detention until their denial of the crime, or alibi, can be verified. In the event that a confession is given or enough evidence is uncovered to incriminate the suspect, he or she is charged with the crime, if there are no extenuating circumstances. Thereafter, the suspect is taken into custody or released on bail.

The case is then prosecuted in court. Many witnesses testify during the trial, giving testimony to implicate or exonerate the accused. When the judge strikes his or her gavel, he or she thereby indicates that the jury should recess for impartial deliberation of the verdict.

The jury may find the accused innocent of the crime, whereupon he or she will be acquitted and released. On the other hand, the jury might find the accused guilty of the crime. The accused is then formally convicted of the crime, sentenced to the appropriate number of years for the violation, and imprisoned.

1)   A criminal case in America
      A. begins when the suspect is sued.
      B. consists of various systematic phases.
      C. is done at the local police precinct.
      D. is dependent upon the seriousness of the crime in relation to the length of questioning.
      E. is dependent upon the police jurisdiction.

2)   Which of the following statements is true according to the passage?
      A. Suspects and witnesses may receive different degrees of questioning.
      B. Law enforcement divisions from various neighborhoods have authority over the case.
      C. Suspects receive more intense questioning than witnesses.
      D. The amount of questioning presented to the suspects and witnesses is standard from case to case.
      E. Suspects normally receive bail.

3)   Witnesses are compelled to
      A. give a sworn statement in court during the trial.
      B. be held in custody while their testimony is investigated.
      C. serve time in detention with suspects.
      D. be prosecuted in court.
      E. be impartial.

4)   After a suspect is charged with a crime
      A. he or she will be required to do time in jail.
      B. he or she will always be released on bail.
      C. he or she may be taken into custody.
      D. evidence is discovered to implicate him or her.
      E. he or she is usually acquitted.

5)   Which of the following statements is false according to the passage?
      A. Once acquitted, the accused will be imprisoned.
      B. If found innocent, the accused is freed.
      C. The accused will be sentenced after being convicted of the crime.
      D. Witnesses may support or contradict the suspect's alibi.
      E. Sentencing and conviction take place concurrently.

Reading Test 12

Archeological Excavation and Interpretation

The discipline of archeology has been developing since wealthy European men began to plunder relics from distant lands in the early nineteenth century. Initially considered an upper-class hobby, archeology in general and archeological field methods in particular have undergone many developments and experienced many challenges in recent years.

Before the field excavation begins, a viable site must first be located. While this process can involve assiduous research, sometimes sheer luck or an archaeologist's instinctive hunch also come into play. A logical locality to begin searching is one near sites in which artifacts have been found previously. Failing that, an archeologist must consider, at a minimum, whether the potential site would have been habitable for people in antiquity. Bearing in mind that modern conveniences and facilities like electricity and running water were not available in pre-historic times, the archaeologist quickly discerns that sites near rivers and caves could provide the water and shelter indispensable for day-to-day living in such inhospitable conditions.

Once the site has been located, the process of surveying commences. This means that the ground surface of the site is visually scrutinized to determine whether any artifacts are protruding through the soil. The archaeologist then digs test pits, small holes that are equidistant to one another, to determine what the boundaries of the larger final pit will be. Once these dimensions are determined, the hole is dug and sectioned off with rope or plastic.

The excavation, which is a meticulous and lengthy process, then begins in full. The archaeologist must gauge the texture and color of the soil carefully as the pit becomes deeper and deeper since variations in soil composition can be used to identify climatic and other living conditions. It is imperative that the walls of the excavation are kept uniformly straight as the dig progresses so that these differences can be identified.

The soil that is removed from the pit is sifted through a sieve or similar device, consisting of a screen that is suspended across a metal or wooden frame. After the soil is placed in the sieve, the archaeologist gently oscillates the device. As the mechanism goes back and forth in this way, the soil falls to the ground below, while larger objects are caught in the screen.

Throughout this process, all findings are entered in a written record to ensure that every artifact is cataloged. This activity can certainly be tedious; yet, it is one that is critical in order to account for each and every item properly. Each finding is placed in a plastic bag bearing a catalog number. Subsequent to this, a map of the excavation site is produced, on which the exact in-situ location of every artifact is indicated by level and position.

Finally, the arduous task of interpreting the findings ensues. During the last two centuries, various approaches have been utilized in this respect. Throughout the early 1800s, most fossil recovery took place on the European continent, resulting in an extremely Euro-centric method of examination and dissemination of findings. Unfortunately, as a consequence, the misapprehension that the origins of *homo sapiens* were European began to take shape both in the archeological and wider communities.

1)   The word *plunder* in this passage is closest in meaning to
      A. take
      B. leave
      C. accept
      D. notice
      E. discover

2)   The word *viable* in this passage is closest in meaning to
      A. collectable
      B. prominent
      C. workable
      D. careful
      E. normal

3)   The words *these differences* in paragraph 4 refer to
      A. climatic conditions
      B. soil variations
      C. excavation walls
      D. dig progression
      E. archeological methods

4)   According to the passage, what do archeologists consider when choosing a potential site for excavation?
      A. whether research can be conducted on the site
      B. whether electricity is presently available
      C. whether the site existed in pre-historic times
      D. whether any data was previously collected from the site
      E. whether the site is well-known

5)   The word *oscillates* in this passage is closest in meaning to
      A. vibrates
      B. exculpates
      C. manipulates
      D. shakes
      E. invigorates

6)   Why are artifacts recorded in a written catalog?
      A. to ensure that no items are lost
      B. to prepare a map of the site
      C. to understand the item's in-situ location
      D. to prepare them for long-term storage in plastic containers
      E. to prevent theft by employees

7) Which of the following statements accurately expresses the author's attitude about the Euro-centric method mentioned in paragraph 7?
   A. It was regrettable, but necessary.
   B. It was completely unavoidable.
   C. It was regrettable because it created cultural misunderstandings.
   D. It only took place within a small geographical area.
   E. It was widespread practice and therefore acceptable.

8) According to the passage, archeological methods
   A. have developed a good deal when compared to earlier centuries.
   B. need to remain static to be useful.
   C. should help to create cultural differences.
   D. have been rectified in countries in the Far East.
   E. vary according to local conditions.

9) Select the sentence below that expresses the main idea of the passage:
   A. An archeologist has many things to consider when selecting and excavating a site.
   B. Protruding artifacts can create difficulties during the excavation.
   C. The excavation of an archeological site is a meticulous and methodical process.
   D. Preparing written archeological records is tedious.
   E. The European archeological discoveries of the 1800s should be disregarded.

This page has been left blank intentionally.

Reading Test 13

Agricultural Production and Processes

Diversification is the key to success in today's agrarian pursuits. Traditionally, farmers have raised livestock such as dairy cows and flocks of sheep, allowing these herbivorous animals to graze in pastures as their primary source of feeding. Today, farmers have augmented their lines of business with the breeding of a wide range of plants and animals.

The breeding of pedigree dogs is one example of the new wave of diversification sweeping the nation. These animals are kept inside kennels, which are usually located in barns or sheds on the premises. Since the dogs are kept in rather confined quarters, it is imperative to be observant of changes in their temperament. A growling or vicious dog may need to be calmed by feeding or petting until it wags its tail as a sign of its contentment.

Another means of widening the scope of production is through the hatching of fish. Several new fish hatcheries have sprung into existence in states such as Colorado and Wyoming. The development of fish is a highly delicate process and must be monitored carefully. The scales, or skin of the fish, must be examined to ensure that they are of the correct color and consistency. The gills must also be looked at to determine whether the fish can respire freely. Additionally, the fins must be scrutinized to determine whether the fish is able to swim properly.

Other farmers have expanded into the area of horticulture. This line of production includes fruit trees, which are raised in orchards on the farmer's property. These trees are deciduous and lose their leaves every fall, at about the same time that flocks of wild birds migrate south for the winter. Evergreen trees, on the other hand, are not deciduous and remain green year-round. Trees such as the spruce, cedar, and pine have become popular for decorative purposes during the December holiday season, making this month an especially hectic time of year for farmers in this business.

Farmers may also wish to use their orchard or grove as a place to keep bees. Even a few hives can produce enough honey to make a tidy profit. Beekeeping does have its drawbacks, however, such as the danger of getting stung by angry or hostile bees.

Whatever line of production is established, cleanliness remains of the utmost importance as no operation will thrive in dingy squalor. All areas must be kept free of the infestation of rodents, especially rats and mice, which may gnaw on trees or attack livestock. Further, methods must be employed for the removal of animal waste. Dung must be disposed of on a regular basis to ensure proper hygiene.

1) In the past, farmers used to
   A. raise cattle strictly for the production of beef.
   B. keep only milk-producing cows.
   C. breed only sheep and lambs.
   D. concentrate their operations on raising grass-eating animals.
   E. take part in various pursuits.

2) Pedigree dogs are
   A. usually kept in places that somewhat restrict their movements.
   B. not carnivorous in nature.
   C. unlikely ever to show signs of aggression.
   D. never in need of human contact.
   E. are usually vicious.

3) Fish must be examined to ensure that
   A. they can inhale and exhale properly through their gills.
   B. their scales are fit for the purpose of respiration.
   C. their fins are the proper shade and texture.
   D. All of the above.
   E. None of the above.

4) The area of horticulture includes
   A. the production of deciduous trees for the holiday season.
   B. the harvest of fruit from evergreen trees.
   C. trees grown in both orchards and groves.
   D. the procurement of honey from beehives.
   E. many financial risks.

5) The problem of hygiene in agricultural environments
   A. may be rectified by the removal of animal carcasses.
   B. encompasses the dilemma of manure disposal.
   C. necessitates a squalid atmosphere.
   D. is solved when all pests have been exterminated through the process of fumigation.
   E. is resolved when rats and mice have been dealt with.

Reading Test 14

Health and Medicine: Current Debates

The question of how to obtain affordable, comprehensive health care is foremost in the minds of many Americans at present. A system of socialized medicine which operates in affiliation with the government is not widely available to the public in America. Rather, it is the responsibility, if not the necessity, of each individual or family to purchase private health insurance.

A patient afflicted with a heart ailment, for example, may find it difficult to afford a by-pass or transplant operation without adequate insurance coverage. To consider a more appalling case, individuals who suffer from contagious diseases, like AIDS, may find the cost of insurance premiums so insurmountable that it might be necessary for them to become wards of the state. Programs have been established by many state governments to deal with these bleak situations.

The dysfunction of the current system has caused the price of prescription medications to skyrocket to an exorbitant level. Any uninsured individual who requires medicine on a day-to-day basis, such as the epileptic for the prevention of seizures, may encounter difficulties in finding a pharmacy to dispense the medication.

Perhaps the most unfortunate victims of the current system are the elderly. It is natural for senior citizens to fall prey to various infirmities during old age, but something is seriously amiss when an elderly patient is discharged from the hospital prematurely to recuperate at home simply because he or she is not adequately insured. Many believe the present system is not beyond reproach. Indeed, some have argued that if the health care system cannot provide care for those who need it most, namely the feeble and frail, it is of no real use whatsoever.

1) According to the passage, the American health system
   A. places the burden of payment for service rendered on the individual seeking medical attention.
   B. functions in alliance with the federal government.
   C. is funded by tax contributions from corporations.
   D. is under scrutiny by various major insurance companies.
   E. is more expensive for families than individuals.

2) Which of the following patients may come across difficulties in obtaining treatment?
   A. a heart patient who does not have sufficient insurance.
   B. an epileptic who has more insurance than required.
   C. a senior citizen who has the correct amount of insurance.
   D. an AIDS patient who is a ward of the state.
   E. All of the above.

3) An individual suffering from AIDS
   A. will probably be required to pay an extortionate fee for his insurance policy.
   B. may become reliant on the federal government.
   C. will inevitably seek financial assistance from national medical agencies.
   D. will receive the best medical treatment under a socialized regime.
   E. will be unable to obtain medication.

4) According to the passage, senior citizens
   A. usually overstay their welcome at the hospital.
   B. are generally virile and strapping.
   C. are admitted to the hospital too early.
   D. are sometimes forced to convalesce at home.
   E. require day-to-day medicine.

5) Which word best describes the current state of affairs concerning the American health system?
   A. subordinate
   B. indignant
   C. amiable
   D. troubled
   E. impecunious

Reading Test 15

Communication in Interpersonal Relationships

In relationships, men and women can behave as if they are from different planets. Sometimes the dynamics of relationships might even lead one to ponder whether the two genders exist in the same universe. Some people are therefore of the opinion that men and women think, feel, and behave in completely different ways. Accordingly, there is a pervasive societal belief in stereotypical roles and phases in romantic relationships.

The initial phase is the first date. Traditionally, a man asks a woman to accompany him to dinner the next day. She accepts and then bustles around to prepare herself. She wants to be gorgeous and charming. He, on the other hand, simply looks in the mirror and shrugs. Of course, he wants to be genial and cordial. Yet, he may have a few misgivings about the frivolous, unsavory, or even despicable events in his past. Upon arriving at her place to escort her for the evening, he may bring flowers as a token of his esteem for her.

When the couple goes out, the conversation may be a little superficial. He tries to be witty, although she might not understand his jokes. She may want to show some affection, but might feel timid because she senses that he is undemonstrative. He sometimes insists on paying the bill so as not to appear stingy.

During the next phase the couple begin to see each other regularly. The relationship may be physically consummated during this time. She tells her friends confidential and intimate details about the relationship. She wonders whether they are destined to be together forever now that they have been united; he wonders who will win the football game on Sunday.

Then the couple have their first serious argument. At this time, either person may become discontented and jeopardize the relationship by misbehaving in various ways. She may accuse him of being immature and insolent, while he might accuse her of being haughty and domineering. She becomes furious and makes some facetious remarks about his appearance. He feels elated to have finally gotten rid of "the old ball and chain."

Several weeks or months elapse. He feels glum. She feels wistful and cannot be consoled. He wonders if there is even a faint hope of her coming back to him. They meet by chance on the street. She says: "I have been so lonely." He replies: "So have I." She alludes to the possibility of a reunion.

Although this should be the part of the story where we say "and they all lived happily ever after," unfortunately things are seldom so straightforward. The bottom line is, if the relationship does continue, it is usually fraught with complexity and misunderstandings. After all, any relationship is comprised of two human beings who are, by nature, imperfect.

1) In relationships, men and women
    A. behave in harmony and unison.
    B. are of differing moral fibers.
    C. usually have little esteem for each other.
    D. sometimes act in ways that are worlds apart.
    E. are stereotypically romantic.

2) During the first stage of the relationship
    A. men are obsessed with their appearance.
    B. women worry about the secrets in their past.
    C. men have doubts about the woman's character.
    D. the couple will go on their first outing.
    E. men are generous and cordial.

3) Which of the following statements is true according to the passage?
    A. Women find difficulty in displaying their emotions.
    B. Men behave with impropriety.
    C. During the first date, conversation is superfluous.
    D. Some disparity exists between the attitudes of men and women concerning relationships.
    E. Relationships are often physically consummated too quickly.

4) When the couple have their first argument
    A. it is usually instigated by the man.
    B. she will give him various blandishments.
    C. he accuses her of being placid and obsequious.
    D. it appears that the relationship is ostensibly over.
    E. they exchange otiose statements.

5) After the break-up
    A. the woman is full of regret, but can usually be comforted.
    B. the man thwarts any attempt to reconcile.
    C. the couple still loathe one another.
    D. the couple may re-unite after a fortuitous meeting.
    E. women experience depression more profoundly than men.

6) According to the author of this passage, human relationships are inherently
    A. deleterious
    B. unstable
    C. lonely
    D. dichotomous
    E. complicated

Reading Test 16

The Westward Expansion Movement

The folklore of the exploration of the American frontier has become more popular than fables or nursery rhymes. Perhaps the popularity of these tales is owing to the mystery surrounding them. It is difficult for us to fathom how these hearty pioneers defied the odds in spite of the exceptionally precarious conditions they faced.

The pioneers traveled westward in covered wagons, which served not only as shelter against the elements, but also as their primary means of transportation, both over land and water. Of course, this method of travel was not without its problems. It was necessary to balance the weight inside the wagon so that it would not tilt when going down the trail. Rain also created treacherous conditions because it could cause the wagon wheels to warp and the covering to sag. If a wagon was left uncovered in a severe deluge, the passengers and its contents would become drenched. In addition, the wagon could develop cracks and crevices.

Their overland journey was very scenic, including lush prairies, jagged bluffs, and rock quarries. While traveling, they often discovered new waterways such as rivers, tributaries, and estuaries. When it was necessary to make a water crossing, the wagon was used as a vessel. A system of buoys did not exist in those days, of course, and some wagons would capsize when floating in the current. In order to prevent this, goods were sometimes hurled to the opposite river bank for retrieval after the crossing. However, on many occasions, it was necessary to jettison some goods into the river. It was usually impossible to salvage these items later as they would get thoroughly soaked.

After a long day, the pioneers set up camp for the night. Their first task was to gather firewood for the campfire. The men would forage for fallen debris, such as twigs, branches, and hollow tree trunks, in the woods. The fire was then ignited by striking two pieces of flint together. When the first flicker appeared, it was necessary to kindle the fire for the purpose of cooking. Victuals were placed in kettles and hung over the center of the fire. The pioneers would squat or crouch around the fire with stooped shoulders, until the fire dwindled to embers and finally cinders. The pioneers then retired for the evening, weary from a long day's journey.

1)   Stories about the American West
    A. have been superseded many times.
    B. are totally incomprehensible.
    C. have not become unpopular over the years.
    D. are generally misconstrued.
    E. are unfathomable.

2)   The pioneers' covered wagons
    A. were obsolete for all intents and purposes.
    B. had manifold functions as well as shortcomings.
    C. remained sturdy after a downpour.
    D. became imbalanced when damp.
    E. were used for hurling objects.

3)   In order to cross a body of water
    A. cargo was often thrown out.
    B. a jetty was sometimes implemented.
    C. it was necessary to submerge the wagon.
    D. goods were hoisted to the other side.
    E. many items were salvaged.

4)   At the end of the day, the campfire
    A. was prepared from forged materials.
    B. was closely guarded to prevent it from being extinguished.
    C. was ignited and continued burning until morning.
    D. usually fizzled out before the meal was prepared.
    E. was put out after eating.

5)   Which of the following statements is false according to the passage?
    A. The journey westward was enervating at times.
    B. The initial chore of the evening was building the campfire.
    C. The wagon sometimes served as a vessel.
    D. The pioneers reveled all night.
    E. American folklore is sometimes shrouded in mystery.

Reading Test 17

Socioeconomic Inequalities: Recent Research

Socio-economic status, rather than intellectual ability, may be the key to a child's success later in life, according to a study by Carnegie. Let us consider two hypothetical elementary school students named John and Paul. Both of these children work hard, pay attention in the classroom, and are respectful to their teachers. Yet, Paul's father is a prosperous business tycoon, while John's has a menial job working in a factory. Despite the similarities in their academic aptitudes, the disparate economic situations of their parents means that Paul is nearly 30 times more likely than John to land a high-flying job by the time he reaches his fortieth year. In fact, John has only a 12% chance of finding and maintaining a job that would earn him even a median-level income.

Research dealing with the economics of inequality among adults supports these findings. Importantly, these studies also reveal that the economics of inequality is a trend that has become more and more pronounced in recent years. For instance, in 1960, the mean after-tax pay for a U.S. corporate executive was more than 12 times that of the average factory worker. In 1974, the average CEO's pay had increased to nearly 35 times that of a typical blue-collar worker. By 1980, the situation was even more dire: the executive's wages and benefits were nearly 42 times that of the average wage of a factory worker. However, in the 1990s, this situation reached a level which some economists have called hyper-inequality. That is, it is now common for the salary of the average executive to be more than 100 times that of the average factory employee. In fact, in the year 2000, most CEOs were making, on average, 530 times more than blue-collar employees.

Because of this and other economic dichotomies, a theoretical stance has recently sprung into existence, asserting that inequality is institutionalized. In keeping with this concept, many researchers argue that workers from higher socio-economic backgrounds are disproportionately compensated, even though the contribution they make to society is no more valuable than that of their lower-paid counterparts. To rectify the present imbalance caused by this economic stratification, researchers claim that economic rewards should be judged by and distributed according to the worthiness of the employment to society as a whole. Economic rewards under this schema refer not only to wages or salaries, but also to power, status, and prestige within one's community, as well as within larger society.

Recently, cultural and critical theorists have joined in the economic debate that empirical researchers embarked upon decades ago. Focusing on the effect of cultural technologies and systems, they state that various forms of media promote the mechanisms of economic manipulation and oppression. Watching television, they claim, causes those of lower socio-economic class to view themselves as apolitical and powerless victims of the capitalistic machine. Of course, such a viewpoint has a deleterious impact upon individual identity and human motivation.

At a more personal level, economic inequality also has pervasive effects on the lives of the less economically fortunate. These personal effects include the manner in which one's economic status influences musical tastes, the perception of time and space, the expression of emotion, and the communication across social groups. The detrimental economic imbalance may at its most extreme form lead to differences in health and mortality in those from the lower economic levels of society.

1) The word *mean* in the passage is closest in meaning to
   A. unpleasant
   B. cheap
   C. basic
   D. average
   E. low

2) Based on the information in paragraph 2, which of the following best explains the term *hyper-inequality*?
   A. The fact that the disparity between high and low level salaries has become so enormous.
   B. The fact that high and low level salaries are bifurcated.
   C. The fact that economists are keenly interested in the subject of financial inequality.
   D. The fact that CEOs have more prestige than factory workers.
   E. The fact that inflation controls salaries.

3) The word *stratification* in the passage is closest in meaning to
   A. paid at a low-level
   B. occurring in pairs
   C. occurring individually
   D. divided into levels
   E. divided into steps of a process

4) The words *that of their lower paid counterparts* in the passage refer to
   A. the inequality which lower-paid workers encounter
   B. the compensation paid to people of lower-level incomes
   C. the salaries of people from affluent socio-economic strata
   D. the benefit to society from the work of lower compensated people
   E. the status of CEO's

5) According to paragraph 4, all of the following are accurate statements EXCEPT:
   A. Cultural theorists have expanded upon the work of previous research.
   B. Television and other media have an effect on social inequality.
   C. Television viewing can reinforce feelings of socio-economic subjugation.
   D. People who view television are more motivated to change their lives.
   E. Economic stratification creates social imbalance.

6) The word *detrimental* in the passage is closest in meaning to
   A. negative
   B. advantageous
   C. antisocial
   D. deathly
   E. noxious

7) Why does the author mention John and Paul in paragraph 1 of the passage?
   A. To emphasize the needs of blue-collar employees
   B. To portray a tragic situation that has occurred in the past
   C. To illustrate the economic effects of social inequality
   D. To describe how poverty has impacted upon the life of one particular child
   E. To explicate hyper-inequality

8) The word *deleterious* in the passage is closest in meaning to
   A. motivating
   B. equalizing
   C. injurious
   D. judicious
   E. impervious

9) According to the passage, which of the following statements best characterizes the personal effects of economic inequality?
   A. Socio-economic status has wide-ranging effects on life and lifestyle, as well as on a number of personal preferences and behaviors.
   B. Socio-economic level primarily affects communication skills.
   C. Socio-economic unfairness results predominantly in lethargy among those most profoundly affected by it.
   D. Socio-economic inequality usually results in premature death to those who experience it.
   E. Socio-economic equality is an elusive dream.

This page has been left blank intentionally.

Reading Test 18

Thanksgiving Day: A Culinary Event

Nowadays, most Americans are too busy even to grab a bite for lunch. But this is not the case on Thanksgiving Day, for this is the day not only to give thanks for bountiful blessings, but also to indulge. Thanksgiving Day is the day to eat, whether food is nibbled or munched slowly, or gobbled steadily.

The preparation of the Thanksgiving Day meal entails many details, including the accommodation of any special dietary requests. So the cook had better get to the grocery store early to avoid rummaging through the larder at the last minute.

When making purchases, the expiration date on the product's flap or label needs to be checked since any stale ingredients will detract from the beauty of the meal. A plump turkey is usually standard, as well as a garnish such as cranberry sauce. Blueberry muffins and apple cobbler may also be served.

In addition, the beverages must not be forgotten. Those wishing to stay teetotaling sober will probably want to serve a non-alcoholic drink such as punch or apple cider. Those who wish to get tipsy, however, would probably rather serve beer or wine. Beer can be served in a tankard to provide enough space for the froth. Wine can be obtained by the cask or bottle, but it is important to remember that difficulties sometimes occur when attempting to remove the cork.

When the meal is complete, there are likely to be left-overs. These can be put in the refrigerator to eat over the next few days. Unfortunately, the kitchen may be left in a grimy clutter with stacks of dirty dishes, and the tablecloth is likely to be stained. Everyone will probably be drowsy after the big meal, however, and may wish to take a little nap. The task of clean-up can easily be tackled the following day.

1) Thanksgiving Day celebration consists of
   A. a quick bite to eat.
   B. only a few morsels.
   C. a variety of confections and refreshments.
   D. a dearth of food.
   E. a culinary nadir.

2) Which of the following statements is false according to the passage?
   A. It is best to plan the feast in advance.
   B. Most people eat greedily and quickly on Thanksgiving Day.
   C. The preparation of the Thanksgiving meal involves many tasks.
   D. It is necessary to peruse the product information prior to purchase to verify freshness.
   E. Turkey is normally consumed.

3) According to the passage, which of the following is not served for the Thanksgiving Day feast?
   A. cocktails
   B. poultry
   C. baked goods
   D. soft drinks
   E. cranberry sauce

4) The drinks served with the Thanksgiving meal
   A. are always intoxicating.
   B. are never fruit flavored.
   C. sometimes include iced tea.
   D. are varied to account for differences in personal preferences.
   E. are only for teetotalers.

5) The Thanksgiving Day feast culminates in
   A. piles of filthy dishes.
   B. immaculate tablecloths.
   C. impeccable kitchens.
   D. sybaritic guests.
   E. All of the above.

Reading Test 19

The State of the Union

Vicissitudes in the political arena are predominant among the events reported by today's press. Stupendous scandals have been uncovered and covert operations foiled as a result of recent media investigations. This may occur after immense and assiduous research into the particular discrepancies among various stories told by politicians or may simply result from an investigative journalist following an instinctive hunch. Had many duplicitous politicians been aware of the menace posed by such journalists, they would have been much more careful in carrying out their subterfuge.

The methods utilized in various scandals and subsequent cover-ups may include bugging governmental offices, tapping telephone lines, classifying documents as "top secret" or purging relevant data from computer systems. Such perfidy towards the democratic process is considered tantamount to espionage or treason by many patriotic Americans.

Once the scandal is uncovered, the politician will be subjected to questioning at a public hearing. Most politicians do not respond with complete candor and servility during these proceedings. However, their testimony is irrevocable and cannot be taken back without committing the act of perjury, or lying under oath. Certain politicians may phlegmatically profess no knowledge of the matter under investigation, while others may coyly state that their recollection of the events is slightly blurry. However, most parties involved will attempt to reply to questioning deftly and resolutely with cogent arguments and apposite remarks.

Ultimately, the hearing is likely to have an adverse impact on the politician's career. During the hearing, the politician may be subjected to daily jeering from throngs of spectators assembled outside the hearing room. The politician may even be forced to relinquish his or her position as a consequence of a unanimous consensus at the hearing, and, thus, be banished from public office for the remainder of his or her career.

1) Political scandals
   A. often come to light due to differences among various versions of stories told by politicians.
   B. are equivalent to covert operations.
   C. are rarely mentioned in the news.
   D. show the magnanimity of politicians nowadays.
   E. follow an instinctive hunch.

2) Disloyal politicians may attempt to
   A. hide secret listening devices in offices and on telephones.
   B. obtain sinecures to avoid responsibility.
   C. exercise more caution in their affairs subsequent to giving up public office.
   D. add irrelevant information to computer files.
   E. respond candidly to interrogation.

3) During public hearings most politicians
   A. answer questions frankly and with clarity.
   B. hesitate slightly before responding.
   C. recall events clearly.
   D. try to reply with appropriate statements.
   E. often commit perjury.

4) The public hearing
   A. may result in the exile of the politician to another country.
   B. may expose the politician to public ridicule.
   C. is poorly attended by members of the public.
   D. Both A & B.
   E. Both B & C.

5) Which statement is true according to the passage?
   A. Most politicians are supercilious in this day and age.
   B. The public hearing may result in the demise of the politician's career.
   C. Testimony can be revised by witnesses as desired.
   D. Most parties reply nervously and hesitantly to questions at the public hearing.
   E. Unanimity is rarely achieved at the hearing.

Reading Test 20

How to Create and Market a Music CD

There are many obstacles confronting recording artists wishing to make an album. If a singer, songwriter, or musician is lured by the quest for fame, he or she had better not have an aversion to hard work as seemingly insuperable snags and setbacks will often beset one's path. Nor is it a feasible notion for the artist to attempt to depend on the album royalties for his or her livelihood because success is often elusive. Musicians need to be diligent and pugnacious, and having some innate talent definitely helps as well.

Recording artists sometimes start off by writing their own songs. At the beginning, lyrics may consist of jumbled or scribbled notes. However, it is helpful for the songwriter to make an official manuscript in order to procure a copyright. This is for the artist's protection as it will provide evidence for legal recourse in the event of the unlawful duplication of his or her work by unscrupulous pirates.

Most musicians try to land an agent. The agent serves as the go-between for the artists and contends with matters such as advertising and publicity. Importantly, the agent also forecasts the demand for the recording artist's work. Even if a band flounders at first, there is no need for despair. Any recording artist can very quickly be inundated by concert offers and selling CD's by the crate.

The agent also introduces the recording artist to a record company, which provides financing for the recording of the album. A specimen recording, called a demo, is made initially to check out the sound quality and viability of the artist. If the demo is successful, the debut CD is recorded in the hushed confines of the studio. Whether an artist is into ballads or rock and roll, the sound must be clear and audible. Any recording tracks of dubious quality, like those with hoarse voices or garbled instrumentation, are rejected as they are certain to be dismissed by both the critics and the public. A cover, which will accurately portray the image the artist wants to project, must then be designed for the CD.

The debut album is finally released to the public for sale. This is the artist's chance to finally test his or her mettle. Sales may flourish. On the other hand, the artist may discover that the sales figure predicted by the agent is exaggerated. The demand for the artist's work may even be totally stagnant. The artist then needs to consider further actions conducive to increasing his or her market share, such as offering free concerts to the public. Above all, recording artists should remember the age-old adage: "If at first you don't succeed, try, try again."

1) Successfully recording an album requires
   A. a dissolute lifestyle.
   B. tenacity.
   C. an attractive personality.
   D. an alternative income.
   E. all of the above.

2) A copyright should be obtained
   A. as a deterrent to illegal reproduction of the album.
   B. only after the original manuscript has been duplicated.
   C. in accordance with the scruples of the band.
   D. to prevent confusing the order of the lyrics.
   E. at the agent's discretion.

3) The role of the agent is to
   A. prevent pirating of the album.
   B. cope with public relations on behalf of the band.
   C. overwhelm the band with business proposals.
   D. provide financing to the record company.
   E. organize tours.

4) The CD recording
   A. is dependent on the support of the critics.
   B. will be followed by the production of a sample recording.
   C. will renovate the band's style.
   D. must reproduce the correct acoustic quality.
   E. takes place simultaneously with the demo.

5) When the record is released
   A. public demand will increase.
   B. market research is conducted.
   C. free public concerts are invariably offered.
   D. the band has a chance to test its courage.
   E. sales booms are experienced.

6) The recording artist may ultimately
   A. fire his or her agent.
   B. re-record the CD.
   C. re-do the cover to the album.
   D. dismiss the critics.
   E. participate in promotional activities.

ANSWERS

Reading Test 1

1) C
2) D
3) E
4) C
5) A
6) E

Reading Test 2

1) D
2) D
3) C
4) D
5) D
6) B

Reading Test 3

1) E
2) E
3) E
4) D
5) A

Reading Test 4

1) B
2) E
3) A
4) C
5) D

Reading Test 5

1) D
2) A
3) C
4) C
5) A
6) C
7) C
8) A

Reading Test 6

1) C
2) C
3) D
4) D
5) C

Reading Test 7

1) B
2) A
3) C
4) C
5) D
6) D
7) B
8) D
9) A
10) A

Reading Test 8

1) E
2) C
3) E
4) A
5) B
6) C
7) E
8) A
9) B

Reading Test 9

1) C
2) D
3) C
4) B
5) A
6) E

Reading Test 10

1) E
2) C
3) A
4) A
5) C

Reading Test 11

1) B
2) A
3) A
4) C
5) A

Reading Test 12

1) A
2) C
3) B
4) D
5) D
6) A
7) C
8) A
9) A

Reading Test 13

1) D
2) A
3) A
4) C
5) B

Reading Test 14

1) A
2) A
3) A
4) D
5) D

Reading Test 15

1) D
2) D
3) D
4) D
5) D
6) E

Reading Test 16

1) C
2) B
3) A
4) B
5) D

Reading Test 17

1) D
2) A
3) D
4) D
5) D
6) A
7) C
8) C
9) A

Reading Test 18

1) C
2) B
3) A
4) D
5) A

Reading Test 19

1) A
2) A
3) D
4) B
5) B

Reading Test 20

1) B
2) A
3) B
4) D
5) D
6) E

Made in the USA
Lexington, KY
10 August 2012